IT'S OK TO BE SCARED!

Written and illustrated by Sue Wright

Dedicated to my Grandchildren
Freddie, Florence, Lee,
Otis, Jessie, Jonjo, Jack,
Gilbert and Sebastian

Text and illustrations © 2021 Sue Wright

ISBN 978-1-9993617-5-4

Forward

I hope that in writing this book, I have given you, as parents, teachers and carers, a tool to explore, a sometimes difficult subject with the children in your care.

We all have difficult emotions, and even as adults we can struggle with them. Talking to children, letting them know that everyone has fears and introducing the concept that thoughts about fears can be objectified and challenged, is a valuable first lesson in healthy mental wellbeing.

Finally, using breathing to calm the nervous system is one of the most useful lessons that all of us can learn.

Sue Wright

Suzie had a problem & she needed help from her older friend Rosie

Rosie knew all about being scared........

I WAS SCARED ON MY FIRST DAY AT SCHOOL BECAUSE I THOUGHT EVERYONE WOULD LAUGH AT ME AND I WOULD HAVE NO FRIENDS

AND Rosie learned from her new friends that EVERYONE is scared of SOMETHING.....

I WAS SCARED OF GOING UPSTAIRS ON MY OWN

I WAS SCARED OF SPIDERS

Rosie's teacher Mrs. Hall told the children that it was a part of their brains that was making them think scared thoughts.

COULD YOU TEACH ME ABOUT THE BRAIN ROSIE?

YES, OF COURSE! LEARNING ABOUT THE BRAIN MAKES WORRIES SEEM SMALLER

Rosie told Suzie about the brain

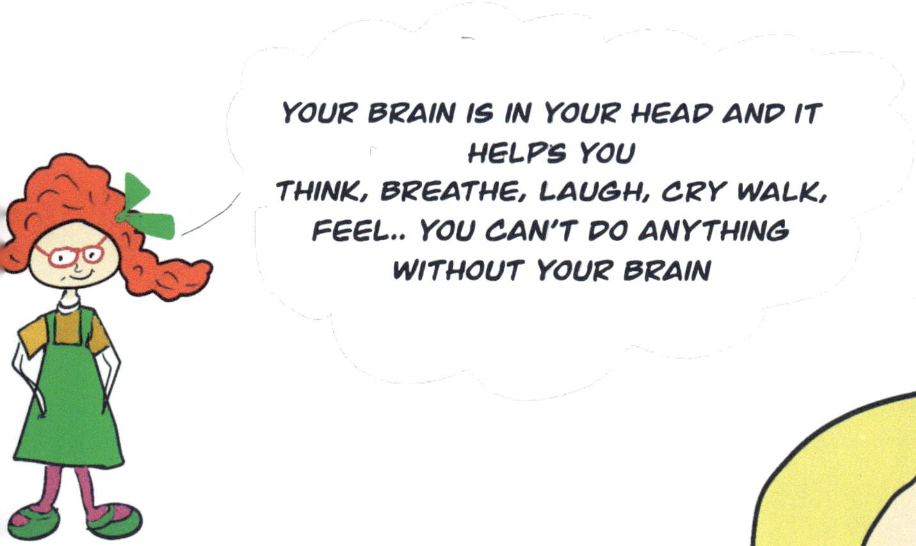

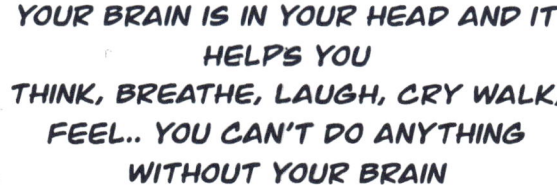

YOUR BRAIN IS IN YOUR HEAD AND IT HELPS YOU THINK, BREATHE, LAUGH, CRY WALK, FEEL.. YOU CAN'T DO ANYTHING WITHOUT YOUR BRAIN

Rosie explained that the brain is a bit like the engine in a car

...but the brain does so much more than help us move. It makes us...

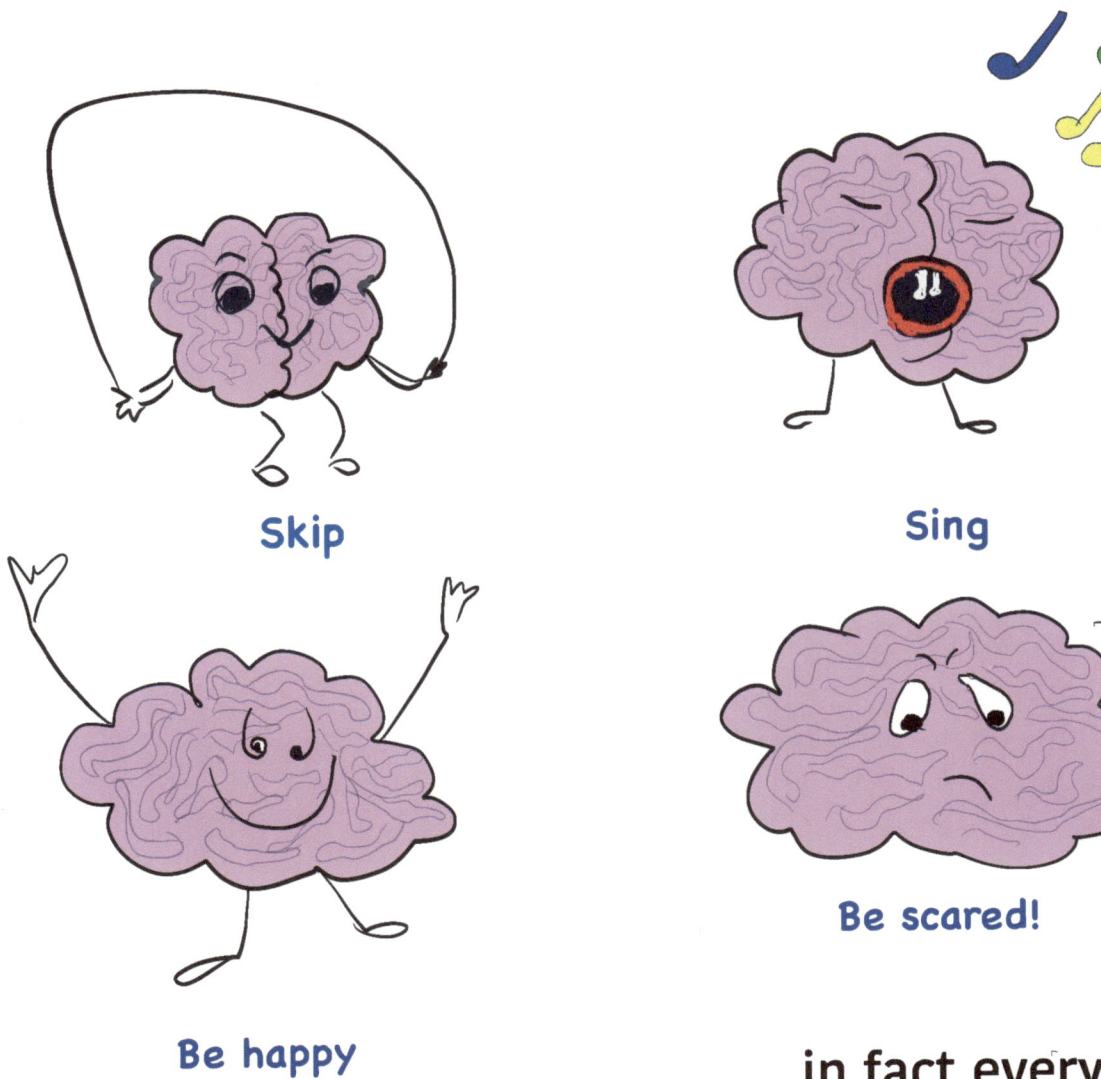

Skip

Sing

Be happy

Be scared!

...in fact everything!

Rosie told Suzie about two very important parts of the brain that help with scared feelings.
First of all meet Guard Dog...

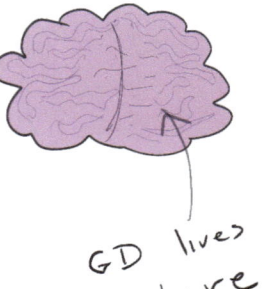

A long time ago people lived in caves.
There were no cars, computers, shops,
schools or TV.

Large creatures lived on the Earth and Guard Dog made children scared of them so they would run away to protect themselves.

The trouble was, the mammoths all went away (became extinct) and poor Guard Dog had nothing to do.

But today there are many dangers for children. Guard Dog realised he had the power to make them scared of these new dangers to protect them from harm

BUT GD STILL MISSED THE MAMMOTHS...

Guard Dog tried so hard to protect the children that he started to believe the mammoths were still there and he imagined other scary things too! He was very happy that he could still protect the children from so many things.

THEY ARE BACK! I CAN STILL BE USEFUL AND PROTECT THE CHILDREN! LET'S PARTY!

but I don't exist GD!

You are confused!

Then along came Wise Owl
(another part of the brain, called Pre-frontal cortex to adults)

OH DEAR, POOR GUARD DOG. HE TRIES SO HARD TO PROTECT CHILDREN THAT SOMETIMES HE GETS CONFUSED AND SEES SCARY THINGS WHEN THEY DON'T EXIST! JUST REMEMBER THAT I AM THE PART OF THE BRAIN THAT HELPS YOU TO ASK QUESTIONS SO YOU KNOW WHEN BEING SCARED IS HELPFUL AND WHEN IT IS NOT!

YOUR BRAIN

Owl lives here!

Questions like....

AND......

...do you remember that Terry was afraid of spiders? Guard Dog trying too hard again...

Malcolm the spider

... and Billy was scared people would laugh at his haircut?

And do you remember June who was scared her colouring wasn't good enough?

Wise Owl told the children that there are things that they can do to stop scary feelings....
Do you want to know what they are?

First - remember it is ok to be scared, but sometimes it is just Guard Dog trying too hard, so shout at your worries to make them go away...

Next... take a deep breath in and breathe out slowly like you are blowing Guard Dog and the scary things far away....

In ... 2 ... 3   out ... 2 ... 3 ... 4 ... 5 ... 6

Then open out your hand and use a finger from your other hand to outline your fingers...

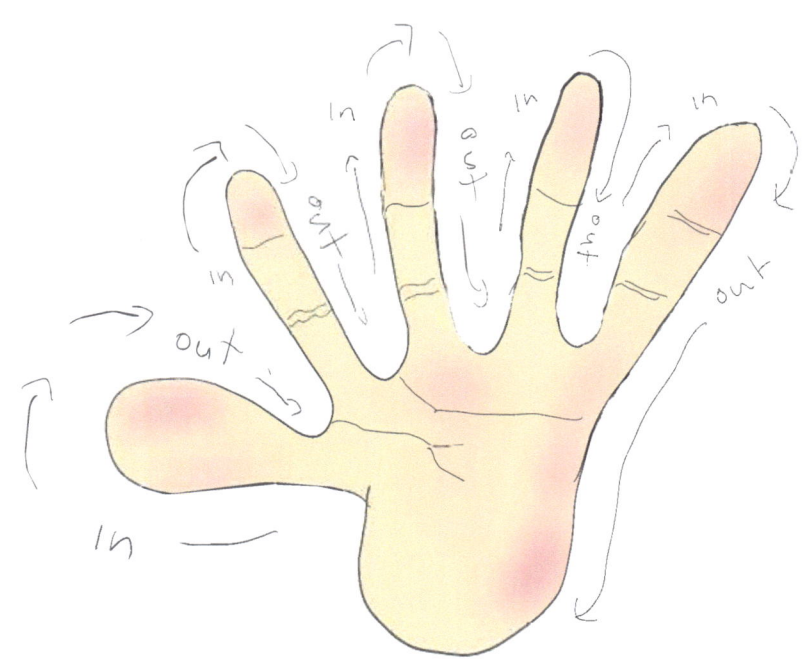

Breathe in as you trace up each finger, and slowly out as you trace down. When you get to your pinky, start once again.

So think what you have to do...

Remember that thoughts might not be true...

Shout at your thoughts and tell them to go...

Sit quietly and breathe slowly...

Use a finger on one hand to outline the other as you slow your breathing for a little bit longer...

Because most of the things that worry us don't even exist!

www.ingramcontent.com/pod-product-compliance
Lightning Source LLC
Chambersburg PA
CBHW040758240426
43673CB00014B/378